POWDERHAM CASTLE

Historic Family Home of the Earl of Devon

INTRODUCTION

Welcome to Powderham Castle, which has been the home of my family for over 600 years. It was built by my ancestor, Sir Philip Courtenay in the 14th century, and, despite many alterations and additions, he and his many descendents would hopefully still recognise it today.

It is an honour to live in such beautiful and historic surroundings, and it gives the family great pleasure to share it with many visitors each year. There is so much to see, enjoy and appreciate that we could never take full value from it ourselves. Nor, frankly, could we afford to maintain it without your help and support.

You are therefore doubly welcome. Each of you is making a contribution to our shared heritage, and we hope that you grow to love and respect what is one of the oldest family homes in England.

Devon

The Castle from the north-east by William Marshall Craig c.1800

TURSDAY
26/8/ 2008

CONTENTS

Lord and Lady Devon enjoy the grounds
of their home Powderham Castle

EARLY HISTORY

EXON DOMESDAY, which survives in the library of Exeter Cathedral, shows that William de Hou, styled 'Comes', held the Manor of Powderham. In the reign of William Rufus (1087-1100) the Manor reverted to the overlordship of the Earl of Hereford. In the reign of Edward I John de Powderham held it, but, when male heirs of that family were not forthcoming, it again passed back to the Earls of Hereford. In 1325, Lady Margaret de Bohun (daughter of the Earl of Hereford) married Hugh Courtenay, 2nd Earl of Devon and Powderham Castle was part of her dowry. On her death in 1391 she bequeathed it to her sixth son, Sir Philip Courtenay, a direct ancestor of the present Earl of Devon.

THE COURTENAY FAMILY TODAY

THE COURTENAY Earldom of Devon goes back to the year 1335 when Sir Hugh de Courtenay, Baron of Okehampton, was summoned to the Parliament of Edward III as Earl of Devonshire. The present Earl is a direct descendant in the male line of the first Earl.

During the Wars of the Roses and the Tudor period, the family lost and regained the title several times until 1553 when Queen Mary created Edward Courtenay Earl of Devon. The present Earl, who succeeded on his father's death in 1998, is 18th in line from the 1553 creation.

The immediate family today consists of the Earl and Countess and their four children. Their eldest daughter Rebecca is married to Jeremy Wharton, with three daughters, Alice, Emelia and Tatiana; their second daughter Eleonora (Nell) is married to Edward Clarkson, with a daughter, Lara, and a son, James; their third daughter, Camilla, is married to Daniel Duff; and their son, Charles, is married to Allison Joy Langer ("AJ").

On the occasion of the English celebration of Charlie and AJ's marriage, 4 June 2005

Back row: Edward, Nell, Charlie, AJ, Lady Devon, Lord Devon, Camillia, Dan, Jeremy
Front row: Lara, Alice, Emelia, Tatiana, Rebecca

HUGH CAPET, 987

ROBERT, 998

HENRY I of France, 1087

PHILIP I, 1059

LOUIS VI (LE GROS) King of France

PIERRE DE FRANCE, seventh son, assumed the name of Courtenay, 1140 = Elizabeth de Courtenay (daughter of Sir Reginald and heiress to his lands in France

PIERRE DE COURTENAY Emperor of Constantinople = Yolande, daughter of Baldwin, Count of Flanders

ROBERT Emperor of Constantinople s.1221-d.1228

BALDWIN Emperor of Constantinople until 1261, died in exile 1273

ATHON, son of the Chatelain of Château Reynard, who fortified Courtenay c. A.D. 1000

JOSCELIN DE COURTENAY 1065 = (2) Isabel, daughter of Milo de Montlhery

MILO DE COURTENAY, brother of Joscelin 1st Count of Edessa = Ermengarde, daughter of Reginald Comte de Nevers, granddaughter of King Robert of France

Sir **REGINALD DE COURTENAY**, Crusader, Baron of Okehampton, Governor of Exeter Castle, came to England in 1152 with Queen Eleanor, wife of Henry II = (1) Hedwige de Donjon (French) (2) Hawise d'Aincourt 'Lady of Okehampton' or her half-sister Matilda (English)

ROBERT DE COURTENAY, Baron of Okehampton, Viscomes Devoniae, Governor of Exeter Castle, d.1242, buried at Tiverton, disseized of his office as Sheriff by Henry III = Mary, daughter of 6th (de Redvers) Earl of Devon

Sir **JOHN DE COURTENAY**, Baron of Okehampton, Constable of the Castle of Totnes, fought in Welsh Campaigns of Edward I, d.1273 = Isabella de Vere, daughter of the Earl of Oxford

Sir **HUGH DE COURTENAY**, Baron of Okehampton, d.1292 = Eleanor Despencer, daughter of Earl of Winton

Sir **HUGH DE COURTENAY**, Baron of Okehampton, High Admiral of the West Seas, created Earl of Devon 1335 by Edward III, d.1340 = Agnes, daughter of Lord St. John

Sir **HUGH DE COURTENAY**, 2nd Earl of Devon, d.1377 = Margaret de Bohun (daughter of the Earl of Hereford and Essex and Princess Elizabeth) whose dowry included the Manor of Powderham which she bequeathed to her sixth son Sir Philip in 1391. Their tomb is in Exeter Cathedral

and 13 other children

Sir **HUGH COURTENAY**, fought at Battle of Crecy in 1346, created Knight of the Garter at the institution of the Order in 1348, d.1349 = Elizabeth

HUGH, d.s.p. 1374

EDWARD COURTENAY of Godlington, d.1371/2 = Emmeline Dauney, daughter of Sir John Dauney, Kt.

WILLIAM COURTENAY Archbishop of Canterbury, d.1396

Sir **PHILIP COURTENAY** 'of Powderham', fought in Spanish War, King's Lieutenant in Ireland 1382-1393, d.1406 = Anne daughter of Thomas Wake of Blyseworth

Sir **JOHN COURTENAY**, d.1419 = Agnes or Joan? Champernowne

Sir **PHILIP COURTENAY**, d.1463 = Elizabeth, daughter of Lord Hungerford, K.G.

Sir **WILLIAM COURTENAY**, d.1485, brother of Peter, Bishop of Exeter and Winchester = Margaret, daughter of Lord Bonville

Sir **WILLIAM COURTENAY**, d.1512 = Cicely, daughter of Sir John Cheney

Sir **WILLIAM COURTENAY**, d.1535 = Margaret, daughter of Sir Robert Edgecumbe

GEORGE COURTENAY, d.1533 = Katherine, daughter of Sir George St. Leger

Sir **WILLIAM COURTENAY**, killed at St. Quentin 1557 = Elizabeth Paulet, daughter of Marquess of Winchester

Sir **WILLIAM COURTENAY**, d.1630 = Elizabeth Manners, daughter of Earl of Rutland

FRANCIS COURTENAY, d.1638 = Elizabeth, daughter of Sir E. Seymour of Berry Pomeroy

Sir **WILLIAM COURTENAY**, created Baronet 1644 but never took out patent = Margaret, daughter of Sir William Waller, celebrated Parliamentary Civil War General, though the Courtenays were ardent Royalists

Colonel **FRANCIS COURTENAY**, d.1699 = Mary Bovey

Sir **WILLIAM COURTENAY**, M.P. for Devon, d.1735 = Lady Anne Bertie, daughter of 1st Earl of Abingdon

TABLE OF DESCENT OF THE COURTENAY
EARLS OF DEVON
FROM ATHON c. A.D. 1000

WILLIAM COURTENAY 1st Viscount, d.1762
= Frances Heneage Ffinch, daughter of Earl of Aylesford

HENRY REGINALD COURTENAY, M.P. for Honiton, d.1763
= Catherine, daughter of Earl Bathurst

WILLIAM COURTENAY 2nd Viscount, d.1788
= 1762 Frances Clack, daughter of Thomas Clack of Wallingford

HENRY REGINALD COURTENAY Bishop of Exeter, d.1803
= 1774 Elizabeth Howard, daughter of 2nd Earl Effingham

WILLIAM COURTENAY 3rd Viscount and 9th Earl of Devon, established right in 1831 to the Earldom created in 1553 by Queen Mary. Died **unmarried** 1835

WILLIAM COURTENAY 10th Earl of Devon, High Steward of Oxford University, d.1859 = (1) Harriet Leslie, daughter of Jane, Countess of Rothes and Sir Lucas Pepys Bt., physician to King George

WILLIAM REGINALD COURTENAY, M.P., 11th Earl of Devon, P.C., D.C.L., Governor of Charterhouse, d.1888 = Elizabeth, daughter of Hugh 1st Lord Fortescue

HENRY HUGH COURTENAY, 13th Earl of Devon, Rector of Powderham, uncle of 12th Earl, d.1904 = Anna Maria Leslie, daughter of Henritta Countess of Rothes

AGNES ELIZABETH COURTENAY, d.1919 = 1869 Charles Lindley Wood 2nd Lord Halifax

EDWARD BALDWIN COURTENAY, D.L., M.P. for Exeter and East Devon, 12th Earl of Devon, d.**unmarried** 1891

HENRY REGINALD LORD COURTENAY Barrister, J.P., Poor Law Inspector for Western District, **d.v.p.** 1898 = Lady Evelyn Pepys, daughter of 1st Earl of Cottenham

HUGH LESLIE COURTENAY, M.A. Oxon, d.1907 = Laura Georgina Courtenay

AMY EVELYN COURTENAY = 1892 Reginald Henry Bertie, youngest son of 6th Earl of Abingdon, d.s.p. 1948

CAROLINE ELIZABETH COURTENAY, d.1935

CHARLES PEPYS COURTENAY 14th Earl of Devon, d.**unmarried** 1927

HENRY HUGH COURTENAY Rector of Powderham, 15th Earl of Devon, d.**unmarried** 1935

FREDERICK LESLIE COURTENAY 16th Earl of Devon, Rector and Mayor of Honiton, d.1935 = Marguerite Silva, daughter of John Silva of Itchen Abbas, Hampshire

EVELYN FRANCIS COURTENAY, d.1985 = 1936 Thomas Anstey, who d.1986

2 sons, 2 daughters

MARY ELIZABETH COURTENAY, S.R.N., S.C.M., who d.2000 **unmarried**

MARGUERITE KATHLEEN COURTENAY d.2003 = 1933 Col. Eugene St. John Birnie, O.B.E., who d.1976 — 2 daughters

CAMILLA GABRIELLE COURTENAY

HENRY JOHN BALDWIN COURTENAY, d.1915

CHARLES CHRISTOPHER COURTENAY, b.1916, 17th Earl of Devon = Countess of Cottenham, born Sybil Venetia Taylor, daughter of John Vickris Taylor of North Aston Manor, Oxford

ANGELA LESLIE COURTENAY = 1947 Harold Cecil Moreton Horsley, M.B.E., who d.1969

2 sons

KATHERINE FELICITY COURTENAY = 1966 Anthony Stephen Pope Watney, who d.1986

HUGH RUPERT COURTENAY, 18th Earl of Devon = 1967 Diana Frances Watherston, daughter of Jack Greenshields Watherston of Menslaws, Jedburgh

MICHAEL HUGH SANDERS WATNEY = 1996 Louise Mary Winsborough

1 son, 1 daughter

REBECCA EILDON COURTENAY = 1994 Jeremy Lloyd Wharton

ELEANORA VENETIA COURTENAY = 2000 Edward Hamilton Clarkson

CAMILLA MARY COURTENAY = 2003 Daniel Bruce Duff

CHARLES PEREGRINE COURTENAY = 2005 Allison Joy Langer

ALICE LUCINDA b.1998

EMELIA ROSE b.1999

TATIANA ELIZABETH b.2002

LARA EILDON b.2003

JAMES RUPERT HAMILTON CLARKSON b.2005

d.v.p. = died before his father
d.s.p. = died childless

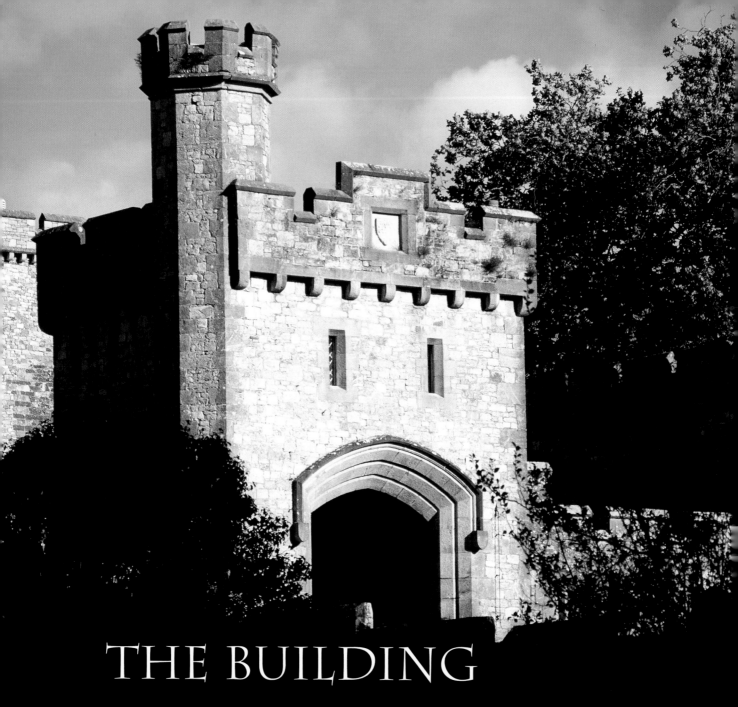

THE BUILDING

THE ORIGIN of the name Powderham is believed to be 'Poulderham', a hamlet on a tidal marsh. It is not known for certain whether there was an earlier building on the Castle site, but as it commanded both the River Exe and the River Kenn, it is likely that there was a tower to guard against invasion from the English Channel

Sir Philip Courtenay began the present building in about 1390. But the most recent additions are first seen as you approach the Castle up the driveway. In Queen Victoria's reign William, 10th Earl of Devon (s. 1835, d. 1859) moved the main entrance to the Castle from the east side, facing the Exe estuary, to the west. This move was probably due to fewer visitors arriving by boat from the Exe. A local Exeter architect, Charles Fowler, was employed for the ambitious remodeling project. He rearranged the Courtyard, building the two Gatehouses and a house for the Steward (now the tea-rooms), and he renewed the entire west front, castellating the skyline and building on the new Dining-Hall to the left of the Entrance Tower.

From the Courtyard the tall rectangular block of the original medieval Castle, which contained the Great Hall, Withdrawing-Room and Kitchens, can still be seen behind more recent additions. The North Tower, at the northern end of the west front, is original and is one of the six towers that Sir Philip built. The Clock Tower on the east side and the Entrance Tower were both rebuilt in brick in the 18th century.

Sir Philip's grandson, another Sir Philip (s. 1419, d. 1463), carried out extensive building works on the east side, adding a Chapel to the north-east wing and building the Grange (the present Chapel) at the south-east end to balance it. The Castle was damaged by Parliamentary forces during the Civil War and lay in disrepair for many years thereafter. As the family fortunes recovered in the 18th century, much work was done both internally and externally, transforming the medieval Castle by the addition of opulent rooms in which to entertain. Lastly came the Victorian alterations mentioned above.

Powderham has always been, and still remains, a family home, to which successive generations of the Courtenay family have made additions and alterations to suit the fashion and needs of their time. This eclecticism adds greatly to its interest and charm. Throughout history to the present day, the Courtenay family has proudly employed local craftsmen and women, artists and architects. The Castle and many of its treasures is a showcase of a unique creativity and craftsmanship born of Devon, but celebrated the world over. Notable contributors include the architect Charles Fowler, portrait painters; Thomas Hudson, Sir Joshua Reynolds and Richard Cosway plus renowned craftsmen such as furniture maker John Channon (Exeter), carpet maker Thomas Whitty (Axminster) and clockmaker William Stumbels (Totnes).

Powderham is also one of the very few great houses in England to have remained with the family who built it for more than 600 years.

N ←——

c. 1390-1450
c. 1710-27
c. 1766-9
c. 1795
19th century

The coats of arms on the wood panelling around the room

One of the carved family coats of arms on the fireplace

Detail from the Family group of Sir William Courtenay of Powderham created 1st Viscount 1762, his wife, Lady Frances Finch, their children and their dogs, by Thomas Hudson

THIS ROOM was built in late medieval style by Charles Fowler for William, 10th Earl of Devon. The interior was completed by his son, William Reginald (s. 1859, d. 1888), who added the beautiful linenfold paneling and the remarkable series of coats of arms, which trace the history of the Courtenay family from its beginnings in France. The series starts with Athon, a French knight who fortified the village of Courtenay to the south of Paris c. A.D. 1000. The French line ends in the 18th century, when this branch died out. The English line starts with Reginald de Courtenay, Athon's great-grandson, who came to England with Eleanor of Aquitaine, the wife of Henry II, in 1154. He married a rich heiress, Hawise d'Aincourt, and through her became Baron of Okehampton, Sheriff of Devonshire and Governor of Exeter Castle. From this couple the English Courtenays descended.

The splendid fireplace was built by the 11th Earl as a memorial to his grandfather who was the Bishop of Exeter from 1797 to 1803. The design is based on the medieval fireplace in the Bishop's Palace in Exeter made for an earlier Bishop Courtenay in 1485. The fire is lit for parties during the winter, especially at Christmas, and throws out a wonderful heat.

There is an historic collection of chairs in the Dining-Hall, including one on which King William III sat for his first Council of State after the Glorious Revolution of 1688. The Council was held at Forde House, Newton Abbot shortly after the new King and his entourage had landed at Torbay. The house was Courtenay property, and the council members were lavishly entertained at the expense of Sir William Courtenay. In a politically conservative move, Sir William contrived not to meet the King in person, thus leaving his options open should the revolution fail! Also of note are two of the late-18th-century brocaded armchairs, which were used by The Queen and The Duke of Edinburgh when they visited Exeter for the Maundy Service at the Cathedral in 1983.

The portraits in this room and throughout the Castle are of family members, and they span the centuries. Two fine Elizabethan portraits hang either end of the fireplace wall, and are attributed to the School of Holbein. On the north wall hangs a huge portrait of William, 1st Viscount Courtenay and his family painted by Thomas Hudson. This is "swagger" portraiture on the grandest scale and it says much about the confidence and status of the Courtenay family in the mid 18th century: they are painted in the finest clothes, in a sumptuous setting and on an unrivalled scale by the most popular artist of the day. As a statement of self promotion, it can hardly be matched. Interestingly the small round table at which Sir William sits is still in the Dining-Hall.

THE ANTE-ROOM

IN THE medieval Castle this was the Withdrawing-Room leading out of the Great Hall. It was redecorated in the 18th century, with the addition of the Corinthian cornice and the rococo ceiling. The fireplace is curious because of the window over it, which was put there in the 19th century when the addition of the Dining-Hall blocked the other outside wall. When the room is in use in the evening a mirror can be rolled across the window. During the last war a young Guards officer was seen one morning gazing pensively at the window. 'How extraordinary', he exclaimed, 'I could have sworn there was a mirror there last night!'

The handsome pair of bookcases is of great interest. They are inlaid with ornately engraved brass in the style of the famous French cabinetmaker André Charles Boulle. They are the earliest known examples of brass inlay work done in England and until their discovery by the experts it was not realised that such work was done in England as early as 1740 and they are signed and dated: 'J. Channon, 1740'. John Channon was a local Exeter cabinetmaker when Sir William Courtenay commissioned these bookcases; he later went on to great success in London, possibly as a result of this commission and the Courtenay patronage. These bookcases are therefore the key to an art historical mystery and they are now the property of the Victoria and Albert Museum, having been sold to the Nation.

Ornate fireplace
with 19th century
window above

THE FIRST LIBRARY

Lady Devon and the Narwhal tusk

THE FIRST LIBRARY was once the drawing-room in which the 2nd Viscount and his large family entertained their guests during the latter part of the 18th century. But appearances are deceptive, for the First Library sits within hidden medieval walls. It was certainly part of the original Castle, and is believed to have been the site of the first Chapel until the 1420 extension.

The room was transformed during the 18th century. The cornice dates from the 1750s. The fine rococo ceiling and the marble chimneypiece were installed by the 2nd Viscount (s. 1762, d. 1788). The bookcases, probably by Avants of Dawlish, mark the final conversion of the room into a library in the 1820s. Together with the Ante-Room and the Second Library, it houses the book collections of the 11th and 12th Earls, which are remarkably untouched and provide a fascinating example of literary interests in the early 19th century. The subjects covered range from literature and science to the classics, but there is a particularly strong emphasis on theology and the collected sermons of eminent clergymen, which illustrates the Victorian Earls' liturgical interests.

Lucy, Harriet and Caroline Courtenay, daughters of the 2nd Viscount, by R. Cosway

It may surprise you to find a narwhal's tusk in the First Library. It is listed in the old inventories as a unicorn's horn, and was believed to possess valuable medicinal properties. Among other attributes it was supposed to detect poison in food or drink by changing colour. At the time when people believed in the magic of unicorns, these horns were rare and immensely valuable commodities: a medieval con-trick.

A book-door leading from the First Library to the China Room, shows one of the Castle's hidden medieval walls

THE MUSIC ROOM

THIS ASTOUNDING room was added by William, 3rd Viscount Courtenay, between 1794 and 1796, and was designed by the most fashionable architect of the day, James Wyatt. Wyatt completed many famous buildings, but perhaps the most legendary was the enormous Gothic folly at Fonthill Abbey, which he built for the notorious William Beckford immediately after completion of the Powderham Music Room.

When they were young, Beckford and the 3rd Viscount, nicknamed "Kitty", enjoyed a scandalous romantic relationship, which disgraced them both. Society did not accept their relationship and they both suffered severely as a result. William was eventually banished and lived out the last decades of his life in unhappy exile in New York and Paris, forbidden from ever returning to his beloved Powderham. But before this tragedy, he built this remarkable room, a timeless legacy that remains and amazes us to this day.

Marbled and gilded pilasters divide the walls with alabaster vases on marble stands in the alcoves between, and the graceful dome is simple but breathtaking in design and provides excellent acoustics. The beautiful chimneypiece was supplied by Richard Westmacott the Elder, Wyatt's favourite sculptor, and is of white Carrera marble. The centre panel shows Apollo and the Muses and the figures on either side are of a Greek shepherd and dancing girl with flute and tambourine.

Elward, Marsh and Tatham, cabinet-makers and upholsterers to the Prince Regent designed the gilt furniture, featuring the dolphin, a family crest. (A bill from them for the years 1797-1799 amounted to £3,000, but was not specific.) The present furniture is a 1990 copy of the original. Thomas Whitty, founder of the Axminster carpet factory, designed the carpet for the room in 1798. The organ, by Brice Seede, is of an earlier date than the room. The 2nd Viscount commissioned it in 1768-69, probably for the new Chapel he had built, and was moved to its present position by Brice Seede's son. There was originally a stage behind where the organ is now placed.

Dancing girl with a tambourine, at the side of the fireplace

William, 3rd Viscount Courtenay
(b. 1768, s. 1788, d. 1835).
Shown in the masquerade dress worn at his
coming-of-age ball. He later became the 9th
Earl of Devon, by R. Cosway

Undoubtedly what inspired William to build the Music Room was his coming-of-age ball, in August 1790. The ball was held in three marquees made of green and pink silk, as there was no room large enough in the Castle for the lavish celebrations. William gave all the 600 guests a peach, an extremely expensive and exotic present, and a very generous gesture. His portrait hangs above the fireplace and was painted in celebration of his coming of age by Richard Cosway, R.A., painter to the Prince Regent and a Devon-born artist. He is shown in his masquerade costume in the manner of Van Dyck, which was the outfit that he wore on the night. The Music Room was used by the Viscount and his sisters for theatricals and concerts and still hosts musical evenings to this day. Some of their beautifully bound books of music can be seen beside the organ, and bills for their music lessons survive in the Castle archives.

According to family tradition the medallions around the walls were painted by the 3rd Viscount and his sisters, who were gifted and well-taught amateurs

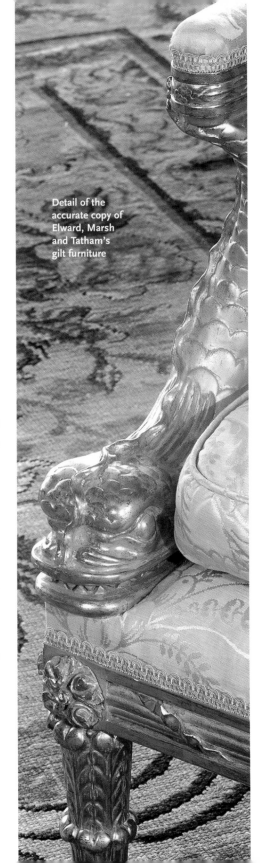

Detail of the accurate copy of Elward, Marsh and Tatham's gilt furniture

THE SECOND LIBRARY

THIS ROOM illustrates perfectly the way in which succeeding generations of the Courtenay family altered the uses to which rooms were put. It was built as a Chapel by the second Sir Philip Courtenay (s. 1419, d. 1463), grandson of the first Sir Philip.

During the Civil War of 1642-1646 the Castle was badly damaged when it was besieged by Parliamentary troops and finally fell on 25th January 1646, and it was not until the early 18th century that Sir William Courtenay (s. 1702, d. 1735) employed John Moyle of Exeter to make it weatherproof.

There is evidence that the chapel was rebuilt and beautified in 1717, but when, half a century later, the 2nd Viscount (s.1762, d.1788) needed more rooms for entertaining, he built a new Chapel where the North Gatehouse now stands and transformed the Chapel on this site into a drawing-room.

THE CHINA ROOM

A SECRET book-door leads from the libraries into what was probably the Guard Room of the medieval Castle, opening into the upper part of the Great Hall. It now houses the family's collection of china, which was in everyday use until 1935, when it was rescued by Lord Devon's grandmother and put on display here. The archway on the right led to the Withdrawing-room, from which a stone spiral staircase led to the upper family rooms.

THE STAIRCASE HALL

THIS IS the upper half of the original Great Hall of the medieval Castle: the part where the Lord of the Manor sat with his family and principal guests, while less important guests and the household sat in the lower half, now the Marble Hall. The partitioning of the Great Hall and the building of the Staircase was part of Sir William Courtenay's restoration of the Castle in the early 18th century, and was completed by 1736, when John Loveday of Caversham, a friend of Sir William's from Magdalen College, Oxford, wrote an account of his visit to Powderham. James Garrett of Exeter supplied the actual staircase with the exception of the heraldic beasts holding the lamps, which are a 19th-century addition. Also in the 19th century, when the Dining-Hall was built, Charles Fowler cleverly adapted the Staircase Hall by filling in windows on the West Wall and cutting out the ceiling lantern, to give the magnificent lighting seen today.

The Staircase Hall at Powderham has been described as "among the half-dozen or so most sumptuous surviving examples of rococo plasterwork in England" and it is remarkably beautiful, with a great profusion of birds, animals, flowers, fruit, foliage, musical instruments and many other objects set against a blue-green background. Until recently the paint was the original and the plasterwork has survived, virtually unscathed, for two hundred and forty years. The principal plasterer was a local man, John Jenkins, with two assistants from London: William Brown and Stephen Coney. The work was begun at the end of 1754 and was probably completed by the spring of 1756. The original estimate was for £217 8s., but in the end it cost £355 14s., plus an extra four guineas for the coat of arms at the bottom of the stairs.

On the bookcase under the stairs there is a figure of Sir Walter Scott by John Greenshields. There is also a marble bust of the 11th Earl as a young man and two swivel guns, formerly mounted at the fore-end of the poopdeck of the Courtenay yacht, the Dolphin, in the late 18th century. Also under the stairs is a canon, one of a set of twelve ordered by the 2nd Viscount in 1775 from T. English of Southwark, as armament for the Dolphin. From this we can surmise that the Dolphin was more than just a pleasure boat and this may go some way to explaining where the family's wealth came from.

The clock on the second landing is by Thomas Earnshaw, chronometer maker to the Admiralty, c. 1740.

The 18th century model frigate

THE SOLAR

THE SOLAR was the family room of the medieval Castle. The fireplace, recently uncovered and restored, is Elizabethan, under a medieval relieving arch. On display are a 1930s doll's house, a selection of family toys including a favourite rocking horse, Dobbin, and an 18th-century model frigate. The frigate is unusual in that it is rigged with complete accuracy whereas the hull lacks much detail. For this reason it has been suggested that it might have been an instructional toy for a boy contemplating a career in the navy.

'Dobbin' the rocking horse still contains his mother's knitting needles, pushed in by Lord Devon's father. Dobbin now rattles when rocked

A section of the
original wallpaper

THE CHINESE PASSAGE

THE CHINESE PASSAGE is
decorated with hand painted
18th-century wallpaper. Like
many 18th century wallpapers it
contains arsenic, which was
regarded as a preservative.
High on the walls are hung the
poles from the last Empress of
China's carrying chair and a
bow-and-arrow, brought back to
this country by an uncle after
the loot of Peking in 1900. The
carrying poles sadly had to be
cut in half for storage on the
ship bringing them home.

25

THE STATE BEDROOM

Detail from the decorative fireplace

THE STATE BEDROOM is situated above the Second Library and contains the ornate bed made for the 3rd Viscount and adorned with dolphins and a Viscount's coronet. The present Earl was born in this bed on 5th May 1942, the day after the Exeter blitz. A certificate of honorary membership of 307 Polish Night Fighter Squadron (Eagle Owls of Lwow) was kindly presented to the Earl, as they had helped to defend Exeter throughout the previous night.

The bed was also featured in the Oscar winning film 'The Remains of the Day'. It was the centerpiece in Lord Darlington's bedroom; however he slept on a camp bed at its foot!

The marvellous Channon bookcases, now in the Ante-Room are believed to have been placed either side of the magnificent classical fireplace, which itself was probably built by the Channon family.

18th century State bed

THE HAUNTED LANDING

The Haunted Landing is so called because, according to an old story, the skeletons of a woman and baby were found in the little room reached by stairs below the Landing.

As the story goes, a carpenter lifting the Landing floorboards uncovered the stairs and it is believed that the woman and baby, who died in childbirth, were sealed in the room where they lay for reasons that can only be guessed at. They were taken to Powderham churchyard for burial. Over the years there have been many reported sightings of a 'grey lady' in the vicinity of the Staircase and Landing, especially when one of the family is gravely ill. Thankfully, none of the present family has seen her.

Decorative phoenix centrepiece from the
last Empress of China's carrying chair

When the late Lady Devon and Mademoiselle Cohard, governess
to the 17th Earl's step-daughters were putting up black-out cloth in
the Castle at the beginning of the last war, they removed some
boxes of shells from the windowsill, took a shutter each and
closed them, went out in the garden and checked that no light
was seeping through - all was well. The following night Lady
Devon went to close the shutters, but found to her astonishment
that they were screwed back against the wall. The house-carpenter,
Arthur Hitchcock, was summoned and questioned as to who
could have done such a thing? Looking rather strangely at Lady
Devon he replied that Earl Henry (the 15th Earl) had had the
shutters screwed back years earlier because they kept on closing
and the housemaids had said they were haunted. When Lady
Devon insisted that this was nonsense as she and Mademoiselle
had shut them the night before, Arthur Hitchcock pointed out that
this was impossible as the screws were rusted in and also there
was a blind (still there), which would have prevented closure. This
was so, and Lady Devon was dumbfounded, for both she and
Mademoiselle were convinced that they had shut them and put
down the bar and the boxes of shells were still where they had
moved them. It remains an inexplicable and strange occurrence.

Many other strange events have been reported in this area. One
day a favourite family dog refused to pass through the doorway
between the Landing and the Lobby, but ran up and down
frantically looking for another way round. Finally, after much
coaxing, it took a flying leap through the doorway, over something,
which it could see or sense and we could not.

The other day, when photographs for this book were being taken,
the Landing was the only place where the photographer had
trouble with his lights. Coincidence? Who can say! The Castle is
undoubtedly occupied by the spirits of many of its previous
occupants, as is any old house. If you are sensitive to them, you
may encounter them.

THE MARBLE HALL

The famous long-case clock, made by William Stumbels of Totnes

THE MARBLE HALL was the lower half of the medieval Great Hall, until it was divided and the staircase built in the early 18th century. It would have been the same height throughout as the Staircase Hall, but now two floors have been inserted. The three original arches leading to the Kitchen, Pantry and Buttery can still be seen, but the arches were faced with plaster at some point and modern doors were fitted in 1844. The doorway in the wall above them gave access to the gallery over the screen at the south end of the medieval Hall and is all that remains of it.

Above one of the arches is a picture painted by the Reverend Matthew Peters of the 2nd Viscount and his wife Frances Clack, with their eleven daughters and one son in 1779. At the time of the painting there were still two daughters to be born!

The fireplace is 18th century, but the overmantel is dated 1553 and is decorated with the Courtenay coat of arms. Over the fireplace a 17th-century Brussels tapestry, after Teniers, shows a farm scene of wonderful perspective.

William Stumbels of Totnes, who was paid various sums totaling £105 for it between 1743 and 1747, made the famous long-case clock. It is of remarkable size and plays a tune for about three minutes at the strike of every fourth hour. It has been suggested that the case may have been the work of the Channon family.

Far left: The Earl of Devon and Dashel by Lucinda Roper, 1998

Left: The Countess of Devon by Lucinda Roper, 1998

THE DRAWING-ROOM

ONE OF THE most attractive rooms in the Castle, this room and the Small Dining-Room to the south of the tower (not shown) were added by the 2nd Viscount when he rebuilt the Clock Tower in 1766. There is a lovely rococo ceiling similar to the ones in the Ante-Room and the First Library. By tradition the two painted cabinets are the work of the 3rd Viscount and the silk behind the marble table that of his sisters.

THE TERRACE ENTRANCE

THE TERRACE entrance, with its lovely views of the Rose Garden, the Deer Park and the Exe estuary, occupies the ground floor of the Clock Tower, where the front entrance to the Castle was situated before it was moved to the west side after 1835.

The two statues are of Coade stone and used to be on top of the gate pillars leading into the Woodland Garden. Coade stone was a form of reconstituted stone, popular in the 18th Century and made by Mrs Coade, but sadly the formula is now lost.

THE CHAPEL

Exterior of the Chapel

THE CHAPEL was consecrated in 1861, but the building is much older. It was the Grange of the medieval Castle and has been dated around 1450. Certainly the hand-hewn timbers are 15th century. As was explained earlier the original Chapel was in the north wing, but when it was turned into a drawing room in the late 18th century another Chapel was built where the North Gatehouse now stands. This is therefore the third and final Chapel, and William Reginald, 11th Earl of Devon, converted it. In his time there was a resident Chaplain and services were celebrated daily.

The monument to the left of the altar is in memory of Elizabeth Fortescue, Countess of Devon, and wife of the 11th Earl. The pew-ends are 16th century. They came from the old church at South Huish and were given to the 11th Earl when he built a new, larger church to replace the old one in 1874.

A beautifully carved pew end in oak

Organ by Bryce Seede c.1800

Christ and his Disciples at Emmaus by R. Cosway c.1790s

THE ROSE GARDEN

Engraving of Powderham Castle c.1740 showing the walled formal garden

ORIGINALLY THERE was a walled formal garden on this side with a Gatehouse in the east wall. By the late 18th century it had been removed and the park came right up to the terrace. The present terrace garden dates from the re-siting of the front entrance in the 1830's.

The 19th-century flowerbeds have all been removed and replaced on a simpler pattern. They contain both modern and old-fashioned roses.

Sundial commissioned by the 1st Viscount from the mathematical instrument maker Thomas Heath in 1750

Powderham Castle
and River Kenn
anchorage
by Buck 1745

... AND VIEWS

IF YOU STUDY the pictures carefully you can see how the views towards the Exe Estuary have changed over the centuries. The sea came very close to the Castle, and following a great storm, flood defence walls were built and the land finally reclaimed, creating the glorious deer park that you see today.

In what must have been a very controversial move, the 10th Earl sold some of the land along the Estuary to The Great Western Railway for the building of the South Devon Railway line by Isambard Kingdom Brunel, changing the face of not only the view but communications, travel and tourism in this part of the country.

Powderham Castle
from the Exe estuary
by Willam M. Craig
c.1800

THE RUNNING OF A MODERN ESTATE

by The Earl of Devon

THE POPULAR view of an English country estate is of a large historic mansion surrounded by numerous tenant farms, whose rents pay for the upkeep of the large house. There may have been past times when this was reality, but it is certainly not the case today. A modern estate, such as Powderham, is every bit a business and needs to adjust and develop with the times to be competitive, economically viable and to remain afloat in the ever-changing seas of fiscal and political policy.

England has an ancient tradition of landed estates and their continued existence is one of the treasures of our cultural heritage. It is due to consistency of responsible ownership and management that England enjoys such a uniquely beautiful landscape.

The Earl of Devon

In feudal times, all land was in the gift of the King. Estates would be granted to loyal and supportive nobility, who could be depended upon to raise soldiers and knights to fight in support of the Crown. During more recent centuries, landed estates were purchased with fortunes made elsewhere, in warfare, trade or business. Estates with large houses were rarely economic and typically they would reduce a fortune through succeeding generations, until eventually the estate was sold to another wealthy owner, beginning the cycle again.

Many of today's surviving estates were founded on fortunes made during the Industrial Revolution and the days of the British Empire. Powderham, however, is one of the minority of survivors from the much earlier feudal era. The Courtenay lands were acquired by Royal patronage, astute marriage and, no doubt, some good old fashioned pillaging in the 13th and 14th centuries. The land at Powderham has consistently been in the family's possession since 1325, which is a remarkable continuity of which we are very proud. One reason for the survival is that the Powderham estate was bestowed in 1391 upon a younger son, Sir Philip, whose successors were not required to take part in the political intrigue and warfare of the late Middle Ages.

The Victorian kitchen

Powderham Castle Gamekeepers c.1880

Powderham Castle Gamekeepers 2005

Thus, when the leading branch of the family was disgraced and their lands forfeited during the 15th and 16th centuries, the Courtenays of Powderham quietly survived.

Irresponsible generations have taken their toll on many ancient estates. In the Regency period especially, though not uniquely, it was not unknown for whole estates to change hands in one evening's gambling and Powderham was lucky to escape a similar fate. In the Archives we have sale particulars dated 1886 for the whole of the 11th Earl's estates, which were drafted to settle his son's debts. Luckily the sale was not enforced and other means were found to satisfy the creditors.

The late Victorian and Edwardian period saw a dramatic downturn in the agricultural economy, which coupled with the subsequent privations of the Great War, saw huge losses to the Powderham Estates and the sale of many outlying farms and possessions, including lands in Ireland. The next generation of the family saw the introduction of Estate Duty, but sadly did not learn the arts of Estate Planning until three brothers had died in quick succession leaving my father, the 17th Earl, with a horrendous tax bill. As with any business, Powderham had to adapt to meet this challenge and, by tightening the belt and diversifying the business, Powderham survived, albeit with its supporting estate much reduced. One of the major steps taken by my father was the opening of the Castle to visitors in 1959, which has been an integral part of the business ever since.

Today agriculture remains one of the primary activities of the estate, though in a very different form to that of twenty years ago. In common with many other smaller estates, the majority of the land is now managed and leased as a single large farm, rather than to a number of tenant farmers. Periodic felling and replanting of woodland produces occasional income and the woods are also used for pheasant shooting. As the pictures show, this has been a pastime on the estate for centuries, but now it is an important element of the estate business. The three gamekeepers also provide valuable wildlife conservation and care for the ancient herd of fallow deer, which is managed for the sale of renowned Powderham venison. The many farmhouses and cottages that previously housed the rural labour-force now provide attractive homes for people working in nearby Exeter and elsewhere.

The continuing urban expansion into the countryside has produced a valuable market to enable the estate to survive and diversify. The creation of the Country Store enables us to market estate and regional produce to the public, as well as providing a year-round destination to meet the demands of year-round tourism. Powderham also enjoys ancient manorial title to the foreshore of the Exe estuary, a popular and very pleasant sailing destination, which enables us to licence moorings and let areas for shellfish farming.

View from the Belvedere across the Exe Estuary with Topsham on the opposite bank

The Belvedere on the hill which overlooks the Castle, and the condition of its interior

Our visitors form part of an expanding leisure and tourism industry, which contributes substantially, though by no means totally, to the maintenance of the Castle and its surroundings. Over the past decade we have developed a successful and highly popular summer concert programme, including a variety of performers from Elton John to Blue and the Bournemouth Symphony Orchestra. Income from the visitor enterprise coupled with Countryside Commission grants have enabled us to undertake a massive project to restore and reopen the eighteenth century Woodland Gardens, the Belvedere Tower and the enormous walled garden, in which all the estate's fruit and vegetables traditionally were grown. These areas had lain derelict for many decades of the last century and it is a joy to be able to bring them back to life and share them with so many people.

As with most estates without large fortunes to exhaust, the position remains that, despite all this activity, Powderham barely generates enough revenue to ensure continued long-term survival in the face of increased maintenance costs, increased intervention by national and local government, and capital taxation. Powderham remains among the great survivors and we intend this to continue. We have plans to develop the wonderful Victorian kitchens and expand our wedding and conferencing business in the coming years, as well as bringing online more attractions for our regular visitors. In doing this, we aim to strike a balance between a necessary degree of commercialisation and the retention of the character of what remains a family home set in its own private estate. We hope that you, our visitors, will think that we are getting it about right.

WILDLIFE ON THE ESTATE

POWDERHAM CASTLE is situated on the Western side of the Exe Estuary, a designated Site of Special Scientific Interest (SSSI). As a result, the wildlife to be found here is varied and spectacular. In spring and summer the Castle is host to many nesting birds such as swallows (12) and martins, spotted flycatchers and grey wagtails. In the grounds there are regular sightings of green and great spotted woodpeckers. In the park beyond our herd of Fallow deer (13) can be seen, sometimes venturing close to the Castle or moving down to the water to drink. The Exe is now home to a significant number of the striking grey heron (10) and now possibly due to warmer winters little egrets (3) from Europe. During spring and autumn ospreys (1) often stop over on migration to feed or rest. In winter the Exe is home to large numbers of waders such as the black-tailed godwit (11) and the avocet, and of course wildfowl, such as the wigeon (6). All of these species can be seen in the vicinity of Powderham. Insect life is prolific due to the biodiversity of the habitats at Powderham and dragonflies, butterflies (17-22) and other insects enliven the gardens and grounds throughout the spring and summer.

1. OSPREY
2. LITTLE OWL
3. LITTLE EGRET
4. CURLEW
5. OYSTERCATCHER
6. WIGEON
7. COMMON TERN
8. DABCHICK OR LITTLE GREBE
9. MIGRANT HAWKER MALE
10. GREY HERON
11. BLACK-TAILED GODWIT
12. SWALLOW
13. FALLOW DEER BUCK
14. COMMON BLUE DAMSELFLY
15. COMMON FROG
16. COMMON DARTER
17. SMALL TORTOISESHELL BUTTERFLY
18. LARGE WHITE
19. PAINTED LADY BUTTERFLY
20. GATEKEEPER BUTTERFLY
21. HOLLY BLUE BUTTERFLY
22. PEACOCK BUTTERFLY
23. BUMBLE BEE

SPECIAL EVENTS

EVENTS are as much a part of Powderham as the Castle and parkland. There cannot be a more perfect setting for a spectacular Last Night of the Proms concert, fireworks, vintage car festival, civil war re-enactment, university balls, weddings and many more.

Each summer the renowned open-air concerts are held. Powderham has attracted performances by many famous stars such as Sir Elton John, Status Quo, Blue, Jools Holland, to name but a few.

We are also able to offer one of the most stunning venues in the country for wedding ceremonies and receptions.

Corporate entertaining and facilities are run hand in hand with the visitor attraction. We hold ride and drive events, seminars, conferences, product launches, and dinners and many other events. We know the Castle always leaves a lasting impression on our corporate clients and their guests.

Powderham is a place full of special memories for so many people; it is wonderful that the events and entertaining business help us achieve that.

ATTRACTIONS -
Something for everyone to enjoy

POWDERHAM really does have something for everyone to enjoy.

The Woodland Garden is a wonderful walk from the Castle and home to spectacular trees and wildlife. In the 18th century the 3rd Viscount and his sisters regularly used it for elaborate picnics. By 1810 the gardens had fallen into neglect and stayed that way until Lord Devon began their restoration in 1994. New trees and shrubs are becoming established and the Mill Leat runs once again.

The Belvedere is also a wonderful place to walk to and enjoy the views of the Exe Estuary and beyond. Completed in 1774 it was used mainly by the 3rd Viscount and his sisters for dances and picnics.

The Walled Victorian Garden is now called the Secret Garden and is home to the many Powderham pets and Courtenay Fort. The Courtenay Fort was built in 2006 by a Cornish company and is very popular with the younger visitors to the Castle and Lord and Lady Devon's grandchildren.

A scenic railway runs through the grounds to the blacksmith and wheelwright. Sometimes the miniature train runs on steam, which is a lovely sight.

THE COURTENAY FORT